Whale Rescue
at Cape Cod Bay

by Belinda Suarez

Glenview, Illinois • Boston, Massachusetts • Chandler, Arizona
Upper Saddle River, New Jersey

One day in July 2002, 56 pilot whales became stranded, or stuck, on land. This happened in Cape Cod Bay, Massachusetts. The whales were close to the shore. It was low tide.

> **Did You Know?** **Ocean Tides**
>
> The tides are the rise and fall of ocean water. At high tide, the water comes toward land and covers more of the beach. Then the water slowly goes down and covers less of the beach. This is low tide.

pilot whale

Pilots whales are dark gray or black.

Nobody knows why the whales were by the shore. Maybe they got lost. Maybe they were looking for food. Maybe they got stranded swimming after fish.

volunteers

Almost 2,000 volunteers came to help the whales. Some were veterinarians, or animal doctors.

Volunteers put wet towels and sheets over the whales. They did not want them to get burned by the sun.

Whales cannot live on land. Their bodies get too hot when they are in the sun. That is why volunteers covered them with wet towels. They also poured water over the whales.

Kids helped too.

The volunteers worked to save the whales. The veterinarians checked them. Everyone waited for the tide to rise.

Finally, the tide rose. The water reached the whales again. Soon they were able to move.

The volunteers helped the whales swim back to the ocean. They made loud noises to scare the whales away from land. They also used boats to chase them away.

Finally, 46 whales swam to the ocean.

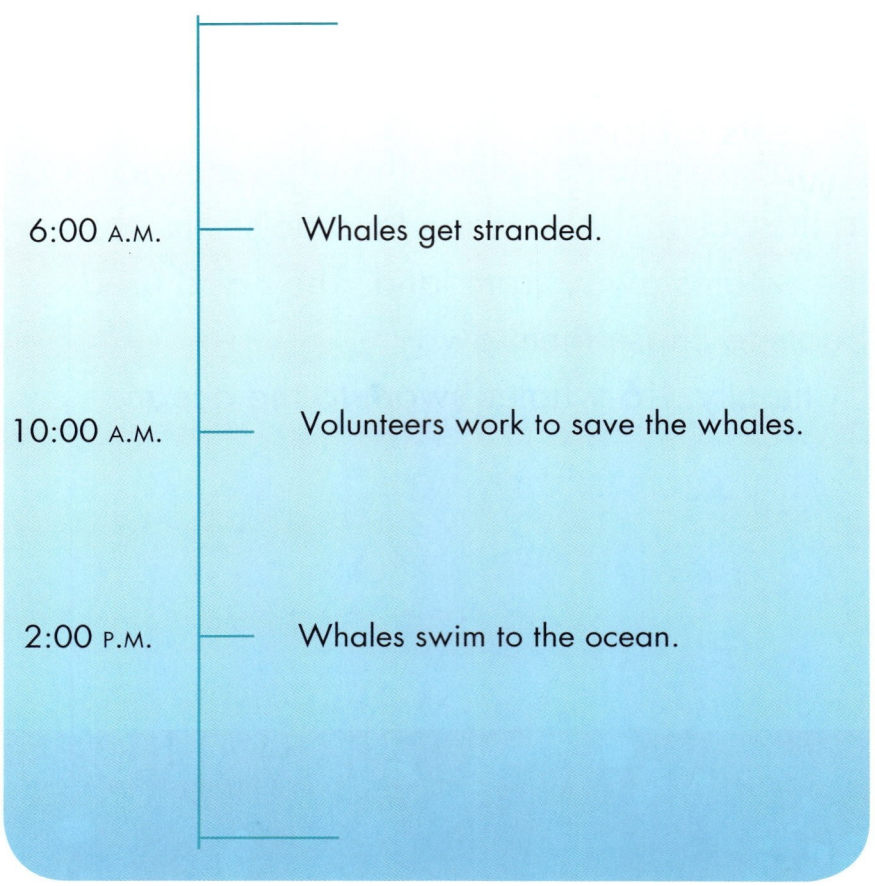

6:00 A.M.	Whales get stranded.
10:00 A.M.	Volunteers work to save the whales.
2:00 P.M.	Whales swim to the ocean.

Can you retell when things happened that day?

This may happen again. Sometimes whales swim too close to land because they are looking for food.

We hope volunteers will always help the whales back into the water.